19 but not 20

By

Alicia Mainor

AuthorHouse™
1663 Liberty Drive
Bloomington, IN 47403
www.authorhouse.com
Phone: 833-262-8899

Because of the dynamic nature of the Internet, any web addresses or links contained in this book may have changed
since publication and may no longer be valid. The views expressed in this work are solely those of the author and do not
necessarily reflect the views of the publisher, and the publisher hereby disclaims any responsibility for them.

Any people depicted in stock imagery provided by Getty Images are models,
and such images are being used for illustrative purposes only.
Certain stock imagery © Getty Images.

This book is printed on acid-free paper.

Scriptures were taken from the King James Version

ISBN: 978-1-6655-1322-7 (sc)
978-1-6655-1323-4 (e)

Library of Congress Control Number: 2021900344

Print information available on the last page.

Published by AuthorHouse 01/25/2021

authorHOUSE®

DEDICATION

I would like to thank God for allowing me to write this book. This book is dedicated to the last 4 years of my life and how it led me to my breaking point in 2019, I could not allow it to continue into my 2020. I dedicate this book to my late parents Charles Mainor and Mary McGee, to my sons Jerrelle and Jaylin, to all my readers and to all of those who had to endure a 19 but not 20 moment.

CONTENTS

Chapter One

PULL OVER

Today I pull over, pray and restart my day. How many of y'all have had to pull over cry and think? It Is My Burnt Toaster and Coffee Time!! With a touch of the Word. Prayer and Direction!! My mom use to say!"

If u let the devil get in the passenger seat in the morning... he will try to ride all day!! So, let me pull over at this next light and open this door and put him out!!!!! Lol he tried it!

This morning!!! But that Sword!!!! (the Word)

I hope everyone started their day knowing God is still shining his light upon us. Do not forget to block the enemy this morning with a simple prayer! Do not let him lead or guide your day into a disaster as I read in Ch.1 King-Vs.9 remember he will bless us with life more abundantly if we keep his commands and laws. You can read it and see for yourself.

I will lead you to it, but you can guide yourself through it.

You have to find it for yourself.

Chapter Two

THIRSTING TO THRIVE

Good morning America ! It's my Burnt Toast and Coffee Time...

The best part of waking up with Folgers in your cup! And a touch of that Word. I hope u guys woke up "Thirsting to Thrive" on this Thursday morning! I wake up Thirsting this Word every morning because this is what lead and guide me throughout my day. This is going to get me through my next season. As I read Ch. Psalms, Vs. 31:1-24 this morning, it put me in check again. I don't know why he led me to this message again, but I trust him to know that it is something in this word I need to know and not forget. And one thing I know is he is my Rock, my Refuge, and my Fortress. He will lead and guide me, then free me from the trap that is set up for me. Knowing I'm not perfect but he loves me enough to not hand me over to my enemies, instead he set my feet in a spacious place.

Read it! Trust it! and Remember it!

You might learn to love it! I hope it grabs you the way it grabbed me.

The word says "Be strong and take heart, all you who hope in the Lord".

This word did not say put your Hope into a man, the lottery, that fancy new car or your new house.

The word of the Lord says *"Put All Your who Hope in the Lord."*

Chapter Three

GOD WILL REVEAL
REMOVE AND REPLACE

I thank God for revealing the things I didn't see, removing the things I wasn't strong enough to remove, and replacing the things I was afraid to lose. Good morning America 🇺🇸. It's my Burnt Toast and Coffee Time!! With a touch of that Word…it is my best part of waking up with Folgers in my cup! This word this morning was awesome. The Lord spoke to me on just what I prayed to him about this morning, it was a great message. I truly needed to be reminded that, I am equipped with all I need to run this race and nobody can stop me not even the devil (a husband on drugs, dysfunctional In-laws, a severe car accident, the loss of my mom and dad, have been lied on cheated on and name scandalized) I was equipped for it all I MADE IT THROUGH . The word said *when the enemies heard you were aware of their plot,* but God frustrated it… he revealed, removed and replaced it. He will frustrate and cancel that plot, curse, or plan that the devil have planned for your life. He will reveal it, rebuke it, and put it under your feet. God gave us "angels" to help us build that wall to block the enemy from getting in our mind, body, soul, our walk of faith, marriage, children, etc. As you read it you see he speak about how they were equipped with armor and was widespread out but still built that wall.

I told u block the enemy in the morning don't let him in, just by chance he get in the passenger seat early in the morning. It is ok just pull over at the next light, open the door and put him out don't let him ride because I promise you, he will try to ride all day.

Reveal Remove & Replace

Feeling Fabulously

Have A Blessed Day!!

Chapter Four

GODS OWN TIMING

Good Morning America It's My Burnt Toast and Coffee Time with a touch of that Word. Today's word comes out of *Ch. 1Samuel 25: Vs.32-44, the word speaks on in Vs. 32:34 how the Lord will send you who and what you need at the right time. He knows what we are thinking before we even think it and will send help at our time of need and he will send us a warning. In Vs.32 David said to Abigail, "Praise be to the Lord "the God of Israel who has sent you today to meet me. May you be blessed for your good judgment and keeping me from avenging myself with my own hands. Otherwise, as surely as the Lord, the God of Israel lives who has kept me from harming you, if you had not come quickly to meet me, not one male belonging to Nabal would have been left alive by day break.Vs.35 The word said : then David accepted from her hand what she had brought him and said, "Go home in peace." I have heard your words and granted your request".*

Now how many times have God sent us a warning or a sign?

For us not to go somewhere or not do something? I know he has sent me a many warnings & signs. I have had 4years of signs and warnings and I thank God today for the 19 But Not 20 warning and signs. I also thank him for taking his hands out of the situation because it led me to a stronger walk with the Lord, because not just me but we all ignore them because maybe we are looking for a direct "Yes or No or Stop or Go." Look how David warning came to him in a form of a woman Abigail, who the Word said that the Lord sent. David recognized that his help came from the Lord, Abigail came to meet him and he said if it had not been for you, he would have killed Nabal by daybreak. Nabal did David wrong but in Vs.38 the word said ten days later the Lord struck Nabal and he died. When David heard that Nabal was dead he said Praise be to the Lord who has upheld my cause against Nabal for treating me with contempt. He has kept his servant from doing wrong and has brought Nabal's wrongdoing down on his own head. Tell me the Lord isn't about his Word, we must know that he has his children his servants as the word said just as he fought David's battle he will surely fight ours. It took him ten days later to do it but he did it. We must learn this word and learn his warnings and signs, he sends to us daily to keep us from making bad choices that could ruin our own lives. God warnings and signs comes in all shapes, forms and fashion.

We must be patient this word teaches us to wait on the Lord as David did. God will show up in his timing not ours just pray and put it in the Lord's hands, he won't allow his servants(children) to fall short. If he did it for David he promise to do it for us. If we line ourselves up with his Word, he will line his self-up with us.

Are you going to fight your own battle and later pay for your wrong doings (jail injured, divorce, ill etc.) or will you pray be patient and wait on the Lord and allow him to fight your battle?

I hear you Lord I'm taking a seat and waiting on you from now on!! Yolanda Adams best sung it and C&S Models best PRAISE DANCED it.

"THE BATTLE IS NOT YOURS"

IT BELONGS TO THE LORDS!

Chapter Five

WHO ARE YOU PRAISING

ood Morning America it's my Burnt Toast 🍞 and Coffee Time ☕ with a touch of that Word📖. Today's word comes out of

Ch. PSALMS Vs. 117:1 short and straight to the point this morning.

It starts with Vs.1 : PRAISE the Lord, all you nations (not some) the word said (All you nations Praise the Lord) (not praise your job or your mom/dad car or man) (it simply said Praise the Lord!)

It continues with:

Exalt him; All you peoples. For great is his love toward us and the faithfulness of the Lord endures forever.

Praise the Lord.

Do you see how we must start and end our days?

the word started with Praise the Lord and it ends with Praise the Lord. To me it wanted and needed to remind us that by God's grace and only by God's grace is how not "Most" of us …the Word said "ALL" of us is making it day by day. its only by God's grace and his mercy that we "ALL" woke up this morning in our right state of minds and able to move ALL our limbs. I don't know about you'll, but I know about me and I thank him and praise him because I can remember when I couldn't move none of my limbs due to a fatal car accident Oh… do I remember and most of you do too. I remember the day in a bad marriage, and I was given the title of my first book "19 But Not 20." I know most of you if not ALL of you have a few "I Can Remember 19 But Not 20 Moments" that it was nothing but God's grace and mercy that brought us through it. Some of us can look as far as yesterday and can say "Praise the Lord" the word said his love and faithfulness endures forever and it does. Just Try him!!

I do not see why it is so hard to try and trust God.

You tried and trusted MAN…and ask yourself this morning who love and faithfulness endured forever? Now let us start this morning over, it is never too late to begin again and it is never too late to Praise the Lord or thank him…let's say it together.

"PRAISE THE LORD".

Chapter Six

LET'S NOT TRY GOD "BUT LETS TRY GOD"

G ood Morning America it's my Burnt Toast and Coffee Time with a touch of the Word.

Today's word comes out of JOB 24:1-25. This word was interesting to me. it came to me in the words of my mom use to tell me as a little girl you might get away but you won't get far or you can do wrong and think because I didn't see you ..just know the Lord sees everything you can't hide under a bush or under a car God is everywhere and he sees everything! Vs.1 says: Why does the almighty (God) not set times for judgement? Why must those who know him look in vain for such days. Vs.2: men move boundary stones.

(do & say what they want) they pasture flocks they have stolen. Vs..3 they drive away the orphans' donkey and take the widows ox in pledge.

Vs..4-11 the word speaks on how MAN (us) does so much wrong & evil. but Vs.12: reminds us how God's love for us is real. Vs.12: the groans of the dying rise from the city and the souls of the wounded cry out for help "But God" charges no one with wrongdoing. this word speaks on all the evil MAN (us) are, will, or continues doing wrong, "to me we just be trying God until he gets tired like in Vs.22 : But God drags away the mighty by his power though they become established,(comfortable in that state of lies killing cheating stealing) they have no assurance of life.Vs.23: He may let them rest in a feeling of security but his eyes are on their ways.(meaning you might get away with the wrongdoing BUT you won't get far he sees it all and as my mom said her mom use to say.. you use to have to go to Hell to pay for your Sins, but some of your Sins & wrongdoing you will pay for right here on earth.Vs.24 says it: For a little while they are exalted and then they are gone. We must stop testing God's love I told you before, yes God is slow to anger as it says in this word .but he does get tired Vs.25: if this is not so, who can prove me false and reduce my words to nothing. you Go God!! Tell us again the word tells us "if this is not so" as to say if I'm lying to the people prove me false(wrong). Take a Look around, take a close look at yourself, then ask is this word lying? Some of us are a living proof to what this word is saying today we all try & test God then wonder or question why? how? what is? or happening to us. Now we know. Vs.23 warns us: it said: He may let u rest in a feeling of security BUT his eyes are on their (our) ways. What are your ways? Let me ask myself Lisa what are your ways? I may be the messenger, but I'm not exempt. let's let our ways mount up to God's ways from this day fourth people.as u see in this word this morning u may have thought you got away but remember you won't get far. God sees it all. let's not end up in Vs.24: for a little while they are exalted and then they are gone .this word this morning is to remind us that it's not too late to get it right get back in God's race so we all can Run on & See What The Ends Gone Be. Who remembers that song? Have a get your ways lined up with God's ways kind-of-day.

Chapter Seven

SELF EVALUATION

Good Morning America it's my Burnt Toast and Coffee Time with a touch of the Word

Today's word comes from Jeremiah ch8: Vs.12-24. The Lord is speaking on in Vs. 1: what man is wise enough to understand this? Who has been instructed by the Lord and can explain it? Why has the land been ruined and laid waste like a desert that no one can cross? Then Vs.13 answered it: The Lord said, it is because they(us) have forsaken my law (word. Commandments) which I set (put gave) before them; they have not obeyed me or followed my law. Vs.14: instead, they have followed the stubbornness of their(our) own hearts.

(Those two verses right there is enough to make u shake your heads because this is what the Lord said not me my mom or my grandma that yes they gets tired of us, and if they can get tired, so can our God. this is what the Lord has spoken pertaining us the people and his children. And how many of us can look back over our lives and say wow God was right? And yes, He has the right to be angry with me and my choices. Because maybe I (we) did follow the stubbornness of our my(own) hearts that lead us in the mess we are in right now today. As we see in Vs.12 it speaks about it, as we think about it, how about ourselves? are we ruined? Ask yourself, are we ruining our kids? Or our own lives? by not following God's word or his commands? instead we choose to follow our own stubborn hearts. Can you answer that today? Does this sound familiar? can you look back and evaluate your life and see whose laws instructions whose directions or advice you followed ? your own or the Lord's?...then ask yourself which one got u (me.) further or closer into our success, better in our marriages, or a better job, and with our health. etc...

Let's have an evaluate ourselves Wednesday.

Chapter Eight

Part 1

THE OX KNOWS HIS MASTER; DO YOU KNOW YOURS (COVID-19 STRUCK A REBELLIOUS NATION)

G ood Morning America it's my Burnt Toast and Coffee Time with a touch of the Word

This word today is good and yet truth rite now today. it starts out with the message saying

"A Rebellious Nation" Vs.1: Hear O heavens! Listen, O Earth! For the Lord has spoken I reared children and brought them up, but they (us we) have rebelled against me. Vs.3: The ox knows his master, the donkey his owner's manager. but Israel (our city nation rite here on earth such as: SE NE NW SW DMV

Area) does not understand. Ah, SINFUL nation a people(us) loaded with guilt a brood of evildoers, children given to corruption! They(we) have forsaken the Lord; they have spurned the Holy one of Israel and turned their backs on him.

I'm going to stop rite there because this much alone is true all we have to do is look at fox5 morning noon & night. This is a must read. We are dealing with such a lost generation but how can the blind lead the blind then ask where can the blind lead the blind? so, it's hard to complain if the parents don't know how will the child if the parents confused full of corruption what do we expect the child to be or to do. Our generation is somewhat just as lost as this up and coming generation. And it's sad to see especially when it doesn't have to be. Why it don't have to be? because I know a MAN a just MAN my God who laid a foundation for u and me and who paved a way who suffered on a cross for our sake and all we have is what we given. We more concerned with black lives matter than we are with the root of to all and that's this WORD God's word his statues his commandments if we could see teach or instill that in a few we just might be a nation that God speak on that Holy nation. All I can read this word this morning and say, "But GOD!" you didn't have to do it, but you did we all fall short I don't know about you this morning but I know the tunes of your grace and mercy brought me threw I'm living this moment because of you want to thank you and praise you too. your grace and mercy brought me threw

Chapter Eight

Part 2

HE IS THE GOD AND
THE WORD IS HIM

G ood Day America it's my Burnt Toast and Coffee Time with a touch of Me going to church
to get fed the Word. And Bishop Staples really put that WORD down at 8am & 10am services
the Word came out of Isaiah 9:6 the message today was "He is God" he is the Word and the Word is
him and he sends his word threw flesh examples, Preachers, Bishops, burnt toast and coffee..etc. This WORD
speaks on how God is the beginning the end the alpha & omega the Prince of Peace a Way Maker a Savior
a Healer a Lawyer in a Court Room a Dr in a Sick room

"He Is God" the one who woke us up this morning in our rite minds and started us on our way kept us
during the night protected us on these streets' highways & byways

"He Is God" and he is worthy to be praised. Vs.6 said: For us a child is born, to us a Son is given and the
government will be on his shoulders and he will be called Wonderful Counselor Mighty God Everlasting
Father Prince of Peace.

Basically "He Is God"

Read Luke 1 threw 24 and see don't you find out about God by December 25th. I dare u to read it I
challenge u to read it.

Chapter Nine
HE HEARD MY VOICE

Good Morning America it's my Burnt Toast and Coffee Time with a touch of the Word Today's Word comes out of PSALMS 116:1-19...This was A real true word today. I really enjoyed this one...Vs.1: I love the Lord for he heard my voice(how many of us today need the Lord to hear our voices) he heard my cry for mercy.Vs.2: Because he turned his ear to me I will call on him as long as I live. Vs.3: the cords of death entangled me, the anguish of the grave came upon me (all our wrong doings) I was overcome by trouble and sorrow.Vs.4: then I called on the name of the Lord, O 'Lord Save Me!. Vs. 5:The Lord is gracious and righteous our God is full of compassion.Vs.6: The Lord protects the simplehearted when I was in great need he saved me.Vs.7: Be at rest once more O' my soul for the Lord has been good to you(us) Vs.8: For you O' Lord have delivered my soul from death my eyes from tears my feet from stumbling that I may walk before the Lord in the land of the living.

That word alone is powerful you must read this word today.it will make a difference in your life.

Chapter Ten

WHO ARE YOU CONNECTED TO?

Good Day America it's my Burnt Toast and Coffee Time with a touch of Me going to church to get the Word. I too need to get gassed up with the Word

get armored up with the Word

get blessed with the Word

get my soul fed and lined up with the Word,

I can't put it out if I don't first put it in. I don't want to run out of gas(the word my power my strength my faith my blessings) by Wednesday(bible study) by Wednesday I might be at a half of tank of the word my faith my walk etc. we must get this word in us daily to lead guide protect direct & correct our paths. the WORD today was awesome at 8am&10am service. this year is built around divine connections. along with healing rebuilding and restoring. the 8am word comes out of Galatians ch6Vs.2. The 10am word comes out of Genesis chapter: 38 Vs.1.After reading this word and hearing the word, my question today is?

Are YOU divine connected to someone who can carry you through difficult times?

Who can carry your burden if it gets too heavy for you?

Who are you divine connected too today?

basically, Can they lead you to heaven or hell?

Can they take action (be committed be all in) when u can't be that for yourself?

Not a cheerleader but a faith leader. I hope we all got a full tank of WORD today.

Chapter Eleven

EVERYBODY THAT CAME WITH YOU CAN'T GO WITH YOU

Good Morning America 📱 It's my Burnt Toast 🍞 and Coffee ☕ time with a touch of the Word📖. Today's WORD was awesome! Today's word comes out of Joshua ch10 Vs.:40-43 (today the Lord has given me a message short and clear. "19 But Not 20" Sometimes we must leave some folk behind. we will have to destroy some friendships or relationships in order to walk with God. This word today in Vs.40: He left no survivors. He totally destroyed all who breathed, just as the Lord,the God of Israel, had commanded.)(wow) (this word isn't like when momma said stay away from that girl or you better leave that boy right there to his momma house, but that one verse our mothers or grandmothers said to us as pups was everybody that came with you can't go with you.. Or everyone cannot go with you to the next level they will surely hold you back.) (So, let us not get discouraged when our friends or family men & women start dropping off and out of our lives. It is not that you are better than them or they are better than you, that just Means it is time to rejoice and thank God for the work he is about to do in you. I thank you Lord right now for my next level. Please Lord show up in our lives today and Remove Replace and Reveal some things in our lives Lord and as you are Removing Replacing and Revealing help us Lord to get Ready for our next level you are taking us to. I ask Lord to please do a work in us today if nobody needs it Lord I DO I am ready for you to take me higher.) Vs.40: So, Joshua subdued the whole region, including the hill country, the Negev, the western foothills and the mountain slopes, together with all the kings. He left no survivors. He totally destroyed all who breathed, just as the Lord, the God of Israel, had commanded.Vs.41: Joshua subdued them from Kadesh Barnea to Gaza and from the whole region of Goshen to Gibeon.Vs.42: All these kings and their lands Joshua conquered in one campaign, because the Lord, the God of Israel, fought for Israel. Vs. 43: Then Joshua returned with all Israel to the camp at Gilgal. (This word was awesome today we need to do an inventory of who or what is holding us back, my questions today are:

why are we still right there?

(how many of us know it is time to move up to the next level?)

(how many of us knows God is ready to take us higher?) But we know we must remove and replace some things and some people and that is what God is waiting for.

And that Is for us to act on his word, I am sure he has revealed some things to us over and over again. Am I the only one who was pushed to "19 but not 20" it could have been he walked out 19 times but it won't be 20 it could be that 19th drink but not 20 it could have very well been that 19th have to get-high but not 20, I've been homeless 19 times or since I was age 19 but not at 20, I have been abused 19 times but not 20, I don't know what your 19 is but not 20 may be only you know, but It's time to start Removing and Replacing so God can take us higher if they aren't walking us towards heaven than they must be walking us towards hell which way are we walking today upward towards our next level that God is trying to take us higher or are we still right there and or walking downward and we all know there is nothing downward but the devil.) Let us get this inventory done today. And decide which way we are walking? Have a blessed day.

In Jesus name we pray

Amen. 19 BUT NOT 20

Chapter Twelve

WHEN WILL YOU LET GO AND LET GOD TRY? I PRAY 19 AND NOT 20

Good Day America 🇺🇸 it's my Burnt Toast 🍞 and Coffee ☕ Time with a touch of the Word 📖. Today's Word was awesome! Today's Word comes out of 1Samuel 16 Vs.. 1-23. (This word was so awesome. It's about being obedient and sacrificing and it speaks on how we must let go and let God trust him and let him lead us and guide us in his direction) This word said in Vs. 1: (basically how long will we worry or fret?) Vs.1: The Lord said to Samuel, "How long will you mourn for Saul, since I have rejected him as king over Israel? (If the Lord said to go, we must go. If he gives his commands we must obey him as that song Said's " I don't believe he brought me this far to leave me") I don't believe I made it to 19 But Not 20 without his grace and mercy and trusting in his word. Yes, he gave me warnings and signs but I didn't step aside I didn't let go and let God be God, and this Word Said's " how long will you mourn for Saul, since I have rejected him as king over Israel? (Watch what it says) (watch the Lord's instructions) Vs..1: cont.: Fill your Horn with oil and be on your way; I am sending you to Jesse of Bethlehem. I have chosen one of his sons to be king.(If God Said's to go we must go we must obey God's commands) (look at what Vs. 2 tells us don't worry nor fret he has us protected in his arms) and I heard it said before that if God told us what we had to endure along the way we wouldn't go. if he just showed us all the trials and tribulations, we must go through just to get to where he is sending us, we would give up stop the race, and throw in the towel. That's why God will just speak in that steel calm voice to go or do or stop he won't give a description of go to the garden or go stand by the tree he will tell us and give us instructions when we get there.) Vs.2: But Samuel said, how can I go? (Wow)

(sounds like us don't it?) Vs.2: Saul will hear about it and kill me.

The Lord said, take a heifer with you and say, I have come to sacrifice to the Lord.Vs.3: invite Jesse to the sacrifice, and I will show you what to do. (Wow) (full instructions) You are to anoint for me the one I indicate. (And guess what? he was obedient) Vs.4: Samuel did what the Lord said. when he arrived at Bethlehem, the elders of the town trembled when they met him. (Feared him) they asked, do you come in peace? Vs.5: Samuel replied, Yes, in peace, I have come to sacrifice to the Lord. (Wow) all I can say is be caught doing what we are supposed to be doing for the Lord. Be about God's work obey his commands let us don't miss our mark when God speaks, we need to be listening. He would not have spoken a word to us if he did not trust us to carry out his plans. I always say God's plan for our life is never our plans for our lives. God may speak a word that May sound un -doable or impossible or may cause our peers friends and foes even our family to laugh and talk negative about but us,but just know God's plans for our lives is never no one else's your gift and your assignment is for you and my gift and assignment is for me so let them laugh chuckle talk bad about us... "I say" just don't give up or give in, TD Jake's was at my church last night and he confirmed a lot for me he said it's between you and God everything isn't for Facebook if God gave you a word an assignment we ought to strike right out on it and know it's between you and Got. He said your close friends won't even understand the calling over our lives and but we must be obedient and know it's between you and God and we must be about Gods business no I'm not saying " as I hear some of us say fast from Facebook" or delete your page take a break all that mess is between us and Facebook and Instagram and whatever we done put up there that caused foolish or crazy reactions or "No likes" but when we about God's work we don't need to be validated or "Liked" or smiley faced and hearted by the world. Because if God said it that settles it and that's validation Liked hearted and smiley faced enough for me. You don't have to like me because my gift from God and enjoying & obeying my god given assignment "I like myself" I don't need validation from the world or fake friends and foes.

trust in God and not in Man learn to cast all our troubles on God and not Man. Our steps are ordered by the Lord not Man. his word said fear no Man .and Remember everybody that came with you can't go with you God has higher heights for us and most of us are holding on trying to stay true and loyal to a dead relationship or a toxic friendship or just because we grew up together and fought together we must Know that God didn't prepare your blessings for you'll it's between you and God.

In Jesus Name We Pray Amen

Have a great evening.

Chapter Thirteen

WHO ARE YOU PUTTING YOUR TRUST IN

Good Morning America it's my Burnt Toast and Coffee Time with a touch of the Word Today's Word was awesome! Today's Word comes out of Isaiah ch8 Vs. 13-22 (this Word today speaks on who God is, this Word said in

Vs. 13: The Lord Almighty is the one you are to regard as holy, he is the one you are to fear, he is the one you are to dread,Vs.14: and he will be a sanctuary; but for both houses of Israel he will be a stone that causes men to stumble and a rock that makes them fall And for the people of Jerusalem he will be a trap and a snare.Vs.15: Many of them will stumble; they will fall and be broken, they will be snared and captured.

Vs.16: Bind up the testimony and seal up the law among my disciples.Vs.17: I will wait for the Lord, Who is hiding his face from the house of Jacob. I will put my trust in him. (Wow) I want to read on, but I got stuck right here...) This word said I will wait for the Lord who is hiding his face from the house of Jacob.(meaning Even though he hears our cry, he heard our prayers he sees all we are going through he knows all about it, yet he still decides to hide his face.). Maybe it is because what we are asking about and praying for, he already knows we are not ready for. If he gives us the house what would we do with it would we still be at the mall trying to keep up with the Joneses or fit in? If he gave us the good husband/wife how would we treat him/her would we cheat not be satisfied complain still hangout with our single unsaved friends would we cook clean would we be a submitting wife/husband?) If he gave us the good paying job what would we do would we still come in late would we call in,would we come in and not want to work would we be envious of our co-workers would we be chit chatting on our cellphone and social media all day? If he gave us the new car what would we do would we stop going to church all 1, 2 or3 services would we be at the car wash Sunday morning? That's just to name a few and this could be why God has hidden his face because we are not ready for the next level we don't want to let go of the past to enter our future that God Has planned for us we are so stuck, the enemy had us as in Vs. 15: many of them will stumble; They will fall and be broken they will be snared up and captured. (Why) because they did it their way) we did it our way we didn't want to do as Vs.17: I will wait for the Lord, (because he is not moving fast enough, see the enemy have us in right now mode instant mode no one wants to wait we go out and Hunt a man down as woman instead of allowing God to have that man of God come find us we so thirsty can't wait she fine he fine scared to be alone and meditate on God let God clean us up inside and out basically make us and remold us to be ready for that husband or wife, car, house or job we just want to show them up and then as this word Said's we stumble we fall and be broken they will be snared up and captured (into the devil's trickery) we must do as this word said in Vs. 16: Bind up the testimony and seal up the law among my disciples. (Basically bind up mount up to This Word stop being bound of This world seal up the law keep this Word tight in our hearts minds and souls seal it up if we have to recite it to ourselves Each day. Just as long as it has us being of Vs. 17: I will wait for the Lord, (let him clean us up mind body and soul and hearts let him teach us to make room for the blessing a car a spouse a house a Job he can't bless us with any of what we ask because we jump the gun and go find or we didn't stop and make room for the blessing how do we make room for our blessings: stop pray listen & wait on the Lord stand still and watch God work it out just look back at our last blessing or our own messing we had a house are we still in it? We had a new car are we still driving it? We had a husband/Wife or two are we still with them? We had a good job or just a job, but we had a job are we still there? (Sometimes we have to be thankful for the small things also). Now ask ourselves why? Then ask ourselves should God be hiding his face from me? Then Why? Then ask ourselves are we doing and living according to his word to receive a blessing? Then why? Am I saved? Then why? Are my besties/ men's-n-nem we hang out with saved? Then why? Are we in a fornicating shacking up smoking drinking lying cheating adultery infidelity situation? Why? Is not all of these things not blessing worthy? Why? But let me tell us what this word says about it: Vs. 19: When men tell you to consult mediums and spirits

(other God's) who whisper and mutter, (we know nothing about it) should not a people inquire of their God? (If we are in doubt, confused, or don't know which way to go, and don't know if this is heaven sent) this word said to inquire their God (Pray and wait on an answer) this word says: Why? Consult the dead on the behalf of the living? (Wow) (basically how can a sinner serving Satan lead us to heaven? (We in the club they in the club we drunk they drunk we are in their bed and they are in our bed, who is leading who to heaven? And if not heaven? Where?) Vs.20: To the law and to the testimony! If they do not speak according to This Word, they have no light of Dawn.Vs.21: Distressed and hungry, they will roam through the land (the streets) when they are famished they will become enraged and, looking upward, will curse their King (the devil) and their God. Vs.22: Then they will look toward the earth and see only distress and darkness and fearful gloom, and they will be thrust into utter darkness. (Wow) I'm just going to Ask us a few more questions (which life will we choose today the light or in darkness?) (Are we going to continue to stumble and fall and be snared up and captured into the devil's trickery?) Or are we going to bind up the testimony and seal up the law? meaning (how he blessed us and brought us out before) Or are we going to do of Vs.17: (I will wait for the Lord, (Eve though I am not ready) I will wait on the Lord who is hiding his face from Jacob.?) And or will we do as this Word says (I will put my trust in him?)

Thank you, Lord for your Word, today. I Pray that your Word touch us and deliver us Today.

In Jesus Name We Pray Amen

Have a Terrific Tuesday.

Chapter Fourteen

WHO OR WHAT ARE WE TAKING REFUGE IN

Good Morning America it's my Burnt Toast and Coffee Time with a touch of the Word Today's Word was awesome Today's Word comes out of Psalms ch31 Vs. 1-24

(This Word today on Christmas Eve is amazing this word speaks on how we must take refuge (a place that provides shelter or protection) in the Lord(How many of us know we need to be asVs.1: In you Lord, I have taken refuge; (I can stop and speak on just that this morning because we all need to take refuge in the Lord if not for ourselves for our children and our children's children but this Word is so awesome today I can't stop right there because the Lord didn't stop right there.) This word continues with) let me never be put to shame; deliver me in your righteousness. (Lord I ask that you please deliver us all today in your righteousness deliver us from us today O'Lord deliver us from over thinking O'Lord deliver us from over spending adding more problems and debt into our lives as we walk into our next season O 'Lord deliver us from sin that may come upon us over the holidays O'Lord) Vs.2: Turn your ear to me,(hear me Lord) hear my prayers hear me as I cry out to you on this day) Come quickly to my rescue; be my rock of refuge, a strong fortress to save me.Vs.3: Since you are my rock and my fortress, for the sake of your name lead and guide me(wow) (who are we allowing to lead and guide us today?) Vs.4: Free me from the trap that is set for me, (How many of us know that the enemy has prepared a trap for us to fail, a trap to do all but succeed, to do all but not trust God's word, a trap to commit sin oh yes the trap has been set for that calling placed upon our lives, Today we rebuke that trap in the name of Jesus we cast it out as in Vs.4: let's speak it together: Free me from the trap that is set for me, for you are my refuge.(Remember there's that word again (REFUGE, it said for you are my refuge: meaning you are my shelter and protection O'Lord) Vs.5: into your hands I commit my spirit, redeem me, O'Lord, the God of Truth Vs.6: I hate those who cling to worthless Idols; (we have to get to that place in our lives to that we hate sinning t we hate holding company with sinners or wicked spirits when that wicked spirit can't stand to be the company of our righteous spirit you know how they use to say I know my mom use to tell me that the Lord and the devil can't stay in the same house, you know the devil got kicked out of heaven..) this Word cont.: to say in Vs.6 : I trust in the Lord. Vs.7: I will be glad and rejoice in your Love, for you saw my affliction and knew the anguish of my soul (look at it: God knows it all, he knows all about us the hurt The pain the stress the depression the suicidal thoughts the loss of a job the homelessness God knows:) it said it right here in his word that's why we must do as this Word said and be glad and rejoice in him at all times good or bad because trouble don't last always: (watch what it say) Vs.7: I will be glad and rejoice in your Love, for you saw my affliction and knew the anguish of my soul.Vs.8: You have not handed me over to the enemy but have set my feet in a spacious place.Vs.9: Be merciful to me, O'Lord,for I am in distress; my eyes grow weak with sorrow, my soul and my body with grief.Vs.10: My Life is consumed by anguish and my years by groaning; my strength fails Because of my affliction, and my bones grow weak.Vs.11: Because of all my enemies, I am the utter contempt of my neighbors; I am a dread to my friends, those who see me on the street flee from me.(How many of us know that you are a dread to our friends and family ?) (Like myself they have dropped off because they were not meant to be in my New seasons I have been made fun of ridiculed name called like the (Church Lady) but God is good and I see them same folk who criticized name called who dropped off along the waist side are still there in the same places still climbing the same walls of destruction) (didn't understand it as to why they don't invite me to party anymore or to hangout anymore or why they slandered my character, I was the fun successful one, too much too lose, life of the parties, (But God) because he had a better plan but through his plan was a process and through that process came some dropping off some folk letting go of some friendship's family ships comfortable places and things and my comfortable way of being, it all had to go and the Lord had to do as this word said I had to become a dread to my friends I had to be the one that Those Who see me on the street flee from me, because they may have come with me but they can't go with me and like most of us, we are fighting, scratching and biting to fit in or to stay in our comfortable places and spaces but to succeed it's going to take un-comfortability, some falls, some setbacks,some let goes, & some hurt, but if we are seeking God with our whole hearts and seeking God for refuge we will walk up out of it without a Kindle set upon us) and I am a witness to that Today as I reached my 19 but not 20 point of my life) Vs.13: For I hear the slander of many; there is terror on every side; they conspire against me and plot to take my life(plot to take our life our peace our joy our Faith our walk, hurt our kids ruin a great family they never had, In the past four years I have seen it all in the leading up to my 19 But Not 20 (Watch this look at what it Said next) (and if I had not kept the faith stayed on my path and followed the word of the Lord as in the next verse I don't know where I would be, all I saw was that the devil was out to destroy me and destroy the God in me(BUT GOD)we must keep this word planted in our hearts

Vs.14: But I trust in you, O'Lord; I say, you are my God. (With that right there how can we fail)

Vs.15: My times are in your hands; deliver me from my enemies and from those who pursue me. Vs.16: Let your face shine upon your servant (in 20/20) save me in your unfailing love.Vs.17: Let me not be put to shame O'Lord, for I have cried out to you ; but let the wicked be put to shame; and lie silent in the grave. Vs.18: Let their lying lips be silenced,for with pride and contempt they speak arrogantly against the righteous. Vs.19: How great is your goodness, which you have stored up for those who fear you. Which you bestow in the sight of men on those who take refuge in you.Vs.20: In the shelter of your presence you hide them from the intrigues of men; in your dwelling you keep them safe (look at God how many know he protects us day in and day out ?)(Who woke us all up this morning and started us on our way, who kept us through the night, a God who not just kept us, this is a God who he kept our kids, our families our love ones safe, as we slept as we drove on these highways and byways as we traveled from State to state as we entered our jobs and entered these malls movies schools and stores, God did it he was our refuge even as we danced in the clubs last night he was our refuge he kept us safe from the intrigues of men (the shooters the robbers the rapist the kidnappers the trafficking the thief of the night which is death, Lord I thank you for your refuge) Vs.21: Praise be to the Lord, for he showed his Wonderful love to me when I was in a besieged city.Vs.22: in my alarm I said, I am cut off from your sight! Yet you heard my cry(though I have sinned and have fallen Short of your glory you still protected me, and had Mercy on me) the word said : Yet you heard my cry for Mercy when I called to you for help.Vs.23: Love the Lord, all his saints ! The Lord preserve the faithful, but the proud (the wicked) he pays back in full .(But on this 24th the last 24th of this year Merry Christmas and Happy New to you all as we celebrate Jesus birthday and enter into our New year and new season 20/20 seeing clearly now that the rain is gone)

Vs.24 said: Be Strong and take heart, all you Who hope in the Lord.

(Lord I thank you for this word on today I ask that you protect us and lead and guide us as you said in your word be our refuge O'Lord deliver us from our enemies O'Lord deliver us from ourselves O'Lord deliver us from over thinking O'Lord deliver from evil Lord protect lead and guide our children O'Lord we will Be Strong and take heart and we will all hope in you. Lord I ask that you heal the sick touch some lives deliver some souls unbreak some hearts mend some marriages break some curses feed & clothe the needy, stretch out your hand upon us all O'Lord and remove all things that are not of you O'Lord Remove Reveal and Replace some things today O'Lord as we move into 20/20 help us to move into it seeing clearly now that the rain is gone,

we weathered our storms 19 times But Not 20

AND LORD I THANK YOU

In Jesus Name We Pray Amen

Have a Terrific Trusting in the Lord Tuesday and a Very Merry Christmas!

Chapter Fifteen

THE DEVIL YOU SEE TODAY YOU WILL SEE NOMORE

ood Morning America it's my Burnt Toast and Coffee Time with a touch of the Word Today's Word was awesome! Today's Word comes out of Judges ch20 Vs. 8-48

(This Word today reminds us that this battle is not yours it's the Lord's (meaning that devil you see Today you will see no more) (that situation we faced that hurt we endured that set back we went through that sickness that illness that depression that financial bind all of those battles we saw in 2019 we will see NOMORE in 20/20. (We've come too far too turn around now. It's not the time to give up. I have too much to lose to turn back now) God didn't give us the spirit of fear he trusted us for the Battle he equipped us for the Battle, he told us in his word that No Weapon formed Against Us Shall Prosper and before we Give up and before we give in, the Lord always steps in right on time and gives us a little more hope to keep on going he gives us the power to not turn back from which we came to not allow that battle to take us down but we take it down as they did in this word they asked the Lord who of us shall go first to fight against the Bejamites? And the Lord replied, Judah go first. (The Lord knows who to send before us, he goes before us the word said if God before us who shall be against us, who shall I fear This Word Said in Vs.8: All the people rose as one man, saying, None of us will go home,No not one of us will return to his house.(If we all walk into 20/20 strong and saying 19 But Not 20 we can't fail, We must all say as for my house we will serve the Lord) if we take back our families and our house and do as this Word said in Vs.8:All the people rose as one man, saying None of us will go home.(Meaning no of us will turn back give in or give up we will All rise as one man and a family as a unit) this Word said in Vs.9: But now this is what we'll do to Gibeah: (we have to have a plan in 20/20) We will walk into it Obeying God's instructions) Vs.10: We'll take ten men out of every hundred from all the tribes of Israel, and a hundred from a thousand and a thousand from ten thousand, to get provision from the army. Then, When the army arrives at Gibeah in Bejamites can give them what They deserve for all this vileness done in Israel.Vs.11: So all the men of Israel got together and united as one man against the city.Vs.12: The tribes of Israel sent men throughout the tribe of Benjamin, saying, what about this awful crime that was committed among you? (We know how we like to question God after he tells us what to or not to do? With our how's? why's? Or what you mean? God questions? We all question him or suggest to him our way like as if he need our help or like he don't know us or know what to do?) (We forget he sees & knows it all) Vs.13:Now surrender those wicked of Gibeah so that we may put them to death and purge the evil from Israel. But the Benjamites would not listen to their fellow Israelites.Vs.15: At once the Benjamites mobilized twenty-six thousand swordsmen from those living in Gibeah.Vs.16: Among all these soldiers there were seven hundred chosen men who were left- handed each of whom could sling a stone at a hair and not miss.Vs.17: Israel,apart from Benjamin,mustered four hundred thousand swordsmen, all of them fighting men.(equipped)Vs.18: The Israelites went up to Bethel and inquired of God they said, Who of us shall go first to fight against the Benjamites? The Lord replied,Judah shall go first.Vs.19: the next morning the Israelites got up and pitched camp near Gibeah.Vs.20: the men of Israel went out to fight the Benjamites and took up battle positions against them at Gibeah.Vs.21: The Benjamites came out of Gibeah and cut down twenty-two thousand Israelites on the battle Field that day. (Wow) we will have some good days and some bad days God never promised us it would be easy but he did promised us he would be there with us) Vs.22: But the men of Israel encouraged one another and again took up their positions where they had stationed themselves the first day.Vs.23: The Israelites went up and wept before the Lord until evening, and they inquired of the Lord.(How many of us has cried wrote all night when we were going through lost hope faith was failing ? And we just cried out to the Lord asking why me Lord? Why do I have to go through this hurt Lord why my child Lord why my marriage fail Lord why am I sick Lord why do I have to forgive them again Lord? Why me Lord?) They said, shall we go up again to battle against the Benjamites, our brothers?

The Lord answered, Go up against them. Vs.24: Then the Israelites Drew near to Benjamin the second day.Vs.25: This time, when the Benjamites came out from Gibeah to oppose them, they cut down another eighteen thousand Israelites,all of them armed with swords.Vs.26: then The Israelites, all the people, went up to Bethel,and there they say weeping before the Lord .they fasted that day until evening and presented to burnt offering to the Lord.Vs.27: And the Israelites inquired of the Lord.(In Those days the ark of the covenant of God was there, Vs.28: with Phinehas son of Eleazar, the son of Aaron, ministering before it.) They asked, shall we go up again to battle with Benjamin our brother, or not? The Lord responded, Go for tomorrow I will give them into your hands. (Don't give up) Vs.29: Then Israel set an ambush around Gibeah.Vs.30: They went up against the Benjamites on the third day and took up positions against Gibeah as they had done before. Vs. 31: the Benjamites came out to meet them and were drawn away from the city.

They began to inflict casualties on the Israelites as before, so that about thirty men fell in the open field and the roads- the one leading to Bethel and the other to Gibeah. Vs.32:While the Benjamites were saying, we are defeating them as before, the Israelites were saying, let's retreat and draw them away from the city to the roads.(Meaning you won't win this battle again Satan) Vs.33: All the men of Israel moved from their places and took up positions at Baal Tamar, and the Israelites ambush charged out of its place on the west of Gibeah. Vs.34: Then ten thousand of Israel's finest men made a frontal attack on Gibeah. the fighting was so heavy that the benjamites did not realize how near disaster was. Vs.35: The Lord defeated Benjamin before Israel, and on that day, Israelites struck down 25,100 Benjamites, all armed with swords. Vs.36: Then the Benjamites saw that they were beaten. (Who is your God?) (I know a God who specializes. How about you?) (We are never alone, if God brought us to it he will bring us through it) it doesn't matter how many times we face this situation this battle, we must always keep in mind that : if God before me who can be against me,if God before me who shall I fear:) this Word said they went up against this battle several times and failed (How many times have we gone Against a battle or situation and failed? (gone to the Dr and got bad news, or received a bad phone call in the middle of the night? battle in

Our Marriage? Battles on Our Jobs? Battle with Our kids? And they all seemed to fail, Why Lord?

"But God" He is always right on time and always right there with us. And he will give us present help. This Word said In Vs. 28: They asked, shall we go up again to battle with Benjamin our brother, or not?

(And look at God response) The Lord responded, Go, for tomorrow I will give them into your hands. (Meaning yes stand on my word, fear not against that battle, don't give up & don't give in. The battle is not yours it's the Lord's. The word said it will be well with the righteous and the wicked will bring disaster upon themselves. so which life which battle will we choose today?) Which life are we going to walk into 20/20? Set a plan now today to walk upright in 20/20 with God.

In Jesus Name We Pray Amen.

It could have been me, it should have been me, if it weren't for the blood. (that song just pierced my soul ... Because it was grace that brought me through. (I am sorry that was a Me moment to thank God) (don't miss your me moment to thank him today)

Have a Thankful Thursday walking in to 20/20?

Chapter Sixteen

PUNISHMENT FOR YOUR SINS

ood Morning America it's my Burnt Toast and Coffee Time with a touch of the Word
Today's Word was awesome! Today's Word comes out of Leviticus ch20 Vs.1-27

"Punishments for Sin"

Today this Word gives us the warning of sinning and the punishment of sinning .we today should know that no sin will go unpunished and that the wages of sin is death it's plain and simple if we work we get wages of pay and that's money. And if we sin, we also get wages of death. It's all here in this Bible in this word we must mount up to this Word today people we must get lined up with the Lord before we cross over into this new year. God spared us and has kept us all year long and the most we can do is thank him for his Grace and Mercy he brought us through and Mount up to his word and let him lead and guide us into our next season.

Because I'm telling you now that we you nor me can make it without him we need him morning noon and night sun up to sun down we need him his love and compassion for us is unconditional we will never find a love like God's love and we need to embrace that love in 20/20 and love him the same as he does us ole' cute Jumbo or that fine piece of woman neither one of them you know who I'm talking about the ones we cater to wake up in the wee hours to travel to see argue with sin for accept lies from mistreated by oh we all know what and who I'm talking about but we all know I am not talking about God because God will never leave nor forsake us he will never lead us astray he will never cause us to sin and all he wants from us is it's right here in Vs.22: Keep all my decrees and law's and follow them, so that the land where I am bringing you to live may not vomit you out.(Wow) (how many of us will vomit ourselves out because we know us and our mess?) (How many of us makes ourselves sick to our own stomach at times?) (Look at what this Word is telling us because if we fill that way about us how do we think God feels about us?) Vs.23: You must not live according to the customs of the nations I am going to drive out before you.(God is removing and replacing in 20/20 and he is letting us know today in This Word that we cannot follow and live like the people of this world the sinners and expect the Lord to bless us . We are a different people and we must stand out we are representing the most high (most of us think we cute or think we bout something anyway so why not think we bout something for God?) This word said we must not live according to the nations (the world the ungodly) those the folk he has Rand is removing who he has brought us out of delivered us from they dropped off let's stop going back to get them they are not meant to go into our next season) this word cont.: to say: Because they did all these things, I abhorred them. Vs.24: But I said to you, you will possess their land: I will give it to you as an inheritance, a land flowing with milk and honey. I am Lord the Lord your God, who has set you apart from the nations.in Vs.26: You are to be Holy to me because I, the Lord, am Holy, and I have set you apart from the nations to be my own.Vs.27: A Man or woman who is a medium or spirits among you must be put to death. (Don't be a follower be a leader just because they are sinning or living ungodly you don't have to do the same. You are to stone them; Their blood will be on their own heads. (If we can't beat them we can't go join them. that's not an option this word said their blood is on their own head. This Word said You are to be Holy to me (why?) because I, the Lord, am Holy (and look at how he thinks of us) and I have set you apart from the nations(apart from the world)(to do what?) To be my own. (Wow) You Go God!!

I don't know who's you are, but I know who's I am and I'm God's own " yes I am.

So, as we walk into our 20/20 let's walk upright in the Lord Knowing who's we are.

In Jesus Name We Pray

Amen

Have a "I will give it to you as an inheritance, a land Flowing with milk and honey." Fabulous Friday

Chapter Seventeen

HE IS AN ON TIME GOD

Good Morning America ▥ it's my Burnt Toast ▤ and Coffee ▭ Time with a touch of the Word ▥ Today's was awesome! Today's Word comes out of Judges ch12 Vs.1-15.

(This Word this evening spoke about how God will step in when we need him. Our battle is already won) this word in Vs.3: let us know that Man will let us down will walk away at our time of need or turn their backs on us in a crutch, But God is our overseer he is always there and this word lets us know to depend only on him, put all our trust in the Lord and we won't fail.) Vs.1: The men of Ephraim called out their forces, crossed over to Zaphon and said to Jephthah, why did you go fight the Ammonites without calling us to go with you? We're going to burn down your house over your head. Vs.2: Jephthah answered, I and my people were engaged in a great struggle with the Ammonites, and although I called, you didn't save me out of their hands. (Wow) when we look for our so-called friends to have our back. We all have been there and who do we always have to call on? Sometimes as in this Word it's best to go alone .some battles and blessings are meant for us to go into alone, because if we have people around, then we will feel that we don't need Jesus and we do. God will allow us to come up on These Battles to show us that he is God and he will never leave nor forsake us he knows all that we are going up against, and Guess what? Though we may feel all alone through that battle, those hard times, that struggle, the hurt, and the pain. I believe all we have to do is Pray call out to God, not look for man, look to God he is our answer to and through it all. We must trust him; you know why we must trust him? Because he trusted us to go through the battle our tough times, our hurt, our sickness,our divorce, out of a job, homeless, in prison, loss of a love one, He trusted us to endure it all, knowing that he equipped us for each and every Battle we come up against . God knew we would not curse him and die. as hard as it was in 2019, we got divorced, we got fired, we lost our homes, we lost a mom or dad or child, but our God still trusted us. But God He still trusted us, that he lifted us, empowered us, saved us, for such a time as this, And I am telling you and myself that we must trust him. If we read this Word it explains just how and why we must trust the Lord, look at it again:) Vs.2: Jephthah answered, I and my people were engaged in a great struggle with the Ammonites, and although I called, you didn't save me out of their hands.(That's how Man will do us) (But look at God) Vs.3: When I Saw that you wouldn't help,(who are we waiting on for help? Man, or God) I took my life in my hands and crossed over to fight the Ammonites, and Guess what? Guess who showed up?) (It said) And the Lord gave me the victory over them.(Wow) that was a two second moment right there) I don't know about you but I know that I need God to show up in my life in my battles today right now and give me the victory over them. (How many of us today need God to show up and give us the victory over our Battles?) This Word this evening is for someone other than myself, I just know it is... unless I'm speaking to some of my perfect friends, some of those perfect Holy folk, I do understand but as for those unperfect set of folk like me, Lord we need you we need you right now,we need you to Bless us with the victory over our situations, victory over the enemy, Lord we need the victory over our own selves over our minds, over our finances,over our lives, over our families, and over our homes, we need you to show up Lord and help us through this battle, help us carry this heavy load that we are carrying Lord, let us not bare this load to & through 20/20 O' Lord.. remove and replace it O' Lord, we need you to do a work in us today O'Lord, Save Heal and Deliver us O' Lord, set us free from the things that has us bound O'Lord, by your strips we are healed O'Lord, I pray Lord that all of our sicknesses, illnesses, loneliness, hurt, brokenness, confusedness, suicidal thoughts, depression, drug addictions alcohol addiction, I pray that every affliction we carry every burden we bare is cast out and removed right now Lord, 🙏🙏🙏❤️💀I rebuke anything that is trying to come Against your people today what the devil meant to destroy us Lord turn it around now we know your Word said what the enemy meant for bad, God made it for our good. Trust him Trust his Word.

Lord we give you all the Glory Honor and all the Praise.

In Jesus Name We Pray Amen.

Have a great Saturday evening.

Chapter Eighteen
LOVE THY ENEMIES

Good Morning America it's my Burnt Toast and Coffee Time with a touch of Me going to church to get the Word Today's was awesome! Today's Word came out of Mathew ch5 Vs.:44. (This Word speaks to a lot of us today (I ask us today) (how many of us know that we are supposed to love our enemy?) (Do we know that in due time we will recover all that the enemy stole from us?) This Word speaks on it Today. And we will recover all. The Lord said it in this Word yes I know it's hard yes I know they have hurt us yes I know they have abandoned us lied on us talked about us yes they have done it all, But God seen it all heard it all allowed it all, I say again, But God just know if God before me who can be against me with God before me whom shall I fear. If we walk into 20/20 with that written on our sleeve we will be well .in this world: Vs.44: But I say unto you, Love your enemies,bless them, that curse you do good to them hate you(how many of us are hated and know we are hated by someone?) (But what does this word speak on that today?) It said: Be good to them that hate you. (Wow) (how many of us are willing to obey God and walk upright in 20/20 loving and caring on our enemies? As God's word said for us to do) (how many?) (I know you giving up the girl bye and whatever's Because she said he said I know I get all that I'm battling with the same thing and about a million of us on this line is battling with the same devil..(guess what?)

But God said in his word today to fix it turn it around turn away from those ways that are sent to destroy our blessings and keep us bound we must let it go and let God in 20/20 and we can't do that holding on to those things and people and ways that are meant to destroy us and that are ungodly let live by his word Today people

Vs.44: But I say unto you, love your enemies, bless them that curse you, do good to them that hate you, and pray for them that despitefully use you and prosecute you. (Why?) (Look at) Matthew 5:45 it says "that ye may the children of your father which is in heaven, for harkened his sun to rise on the evil and on the good, And sendeth rain on the just and the unjust". That's just how much God loves us all so let's pray for those who despitefully hurt us or use us God will use our enemies as our footstools if we just be still obey his word and walk upright and just. And love everybody. remember we all were Sinners serving Satan just because some of us might wear a collar now or a fancy dress or stand in that pulpit instead of on that altar every Sunday weeping don't mean we got it all together we are all a work in progress God is doing a work in us all. We all need a little pushing and shoving sometimes we didn't just stop God stopped us. We didn't do it or get it (saved and filled with the Holy ghost and baptized in the name of the father the son and the Holy ghost) on our own no we didn't so let's help our enemies get there just as someone helped us get there. Let's not talk about folk let's try Praying for them laying hands on them speaking life into them. And believe me God will pour out a blessing the same blessing you pour out of yourself for our enemies and others.

We will recover all in 20/20.

In Jesus Name We Pray Amen

Have a Wonderful Sunday

Chapter Nineteen

19 BUT NOT 20

ood Morning America  it's my Burnt Toast and Coffee Time with a touch of the Word Today's Word was awesome Today's Word comes out of Psalms ch5 Vs.:1-12 (this Word today speaks on how we must wake up every morning with God on our minds,a hymn in our hearts thanking God for his Grace and Mercy and for keeping us and our family throughout the night because somebody didn't make it this morning, somebody woke up hurt and or angry this morning, somebody woke up with a sickness in their bodies this morning, and some woke up not in their rightful mind.. so yes, we truly have to wake up and give God thanks and pray out to him for just another day because he didn't have to do it, but he did. he gave us another day to get it right with him and for that alone Lord I thank you. I know I am not alone with the praise and all the Honor to you this morning, So I want to say thank you for your Grace and Mercy that brought us through, We are living this moment because of you. The song say: I want to Praise you and thank you too... your Grace and Mercy brought us through. And I will go on to say I want to thank you for saving a wretch like me. (I *tell you people when it comes down to God, I can talk about him all day because he has done so much for me that I just can't tell it all*). But this Word tells it all in Vs. 7: it said: But I, by your great Mercy, will come into your house; in reverence will I bow down toward your Holy Temple. Vs.8: Lead me, O'Lord, in your righteousness Because of my enemies make straight your way before me. (Meaning direct my path, go before me O'Lord, clear my path for me, remove and protect me from my enemies O'Lord. This word said in Vs.1: Give ear to my words, O'Lord, consider my sighing. Vs.2: Listen to my cry for help, my King, and my God, for to you I pray. Vs.3: In the morning, O'Lord, you hear my voice; in the morning I lay my request before you and wait in expectation. Vs.4: You are not a God who takes pleasure in evil; with you the wicked cannot stand in your presence; you hate all who do wrong.(Now if we didn't know, we know today that God hate, he does not like, he does not take any pleasure in evil (sinning : lying adultery infidelity stealing idling other God's or killing) this Word just told us how our God feels about these things and God only helps fools and babies and as of today under the sound of this message neither you nor myself are fools ..so it's time to not be hated or unpleasured by God but to be loved and pleasured by him. We want to dwell in the Lord and this Word said that with you the wicked cannot dwell. The arrogant cannot stand in his presence; (it say in) Vs. 5: you hate all who do wrong's: Vs.6 You destroy those who tell lies; bloodthirsty and deceitful men the Lord abhors. Vs.7: But I, by your great Mercy, will come into your house; in reverence will I bow down toward your Holy Temple.Vs.8: Lead me, O'Lord, in your righteousness Because of my enemies make straight your way before me. Vs.9: Not a word from their mouth can be trusted; their heart is filled with destruction. Their throat is an open grave; with their tongue they speak deceit. Vs.10: Declare them guilty, O God! Let their intrigues be their downfall., Banish them for their many sins, for they have rebelled against you. (Won't No Sin Go Unpunished) Vs.11: But let all who take refuge in you be glad; let them ever sing for Joy. Spread your protection over them, that Those Who love your name may rejoice in you. Vs.12: for Surely, O'Lord, you bless the righteous; you surround them with your favor as with a shield.

(Lord I thank you for your Word on today I ask that you Lead and guide us into our next season our next year with peace and joy allowing nothing to hinder our walk, or your plan set upon our lives. Lord we thank you for your power, we thank you for giving us a peace of mind, we thank you for your messenger on this morning, we thank you for your present help at our time of need, we are thanking you for giving us another day to get it right, we thank you for allowing us to see another day on this Earth, Lord have your way today let your will be done and not ours and as we walk into 20/20 Lord clear our paths O'Lord go before us O'Lord, we know 2019 was a ruff season for most of us but we thank you for the rough times Lord we know it's all going to work out for our good it was preparing us molding and shaping us to be great & strong to withstand what's in our next season to come. So, Lord we thank you because you were with us throughout it all.

(And I will repeat it)

It was your Grace and Mercy that brought Me(us) through.

I'm living this moment because of you; I want to thank you and praise you too. because your Grace and Mercy brought me through.

In Jesus Name We Pray Amen

Let's Have a

"In The Morning", O'Lord, You Hear My Voice.

"In The Morning"

I Lay My Requests Before You And Wait In Expectation.

Marvelous Monday.

I WAS UNFAITHFUL

I JOINED MY HUSBAND IN OUR BACKYARD, HE WAS CUTTING THE LAWN, I ASKED HIM TO COME SIT DOWN FOR A CUP OF TEA, AS HE DRANK HIS TEA,I LOOKED AT HIM AND SAID I HAVE SOMETHING I NEED TO CONFESS TO YOU, HE SAID WHATS WRONG BABY? TALK TO ME, I THEN TOLD HIM, I HAVE BEEN UNFAITHFUL. MY HUSBAND LOOKED AT ME WITH ANGER AND HURT ALL OVER HIS FACE, HE STOOD UP AND PUSHED THE PICNIC TABLE OVER AND GOT IN MY FACE, AND SAID HOW COULD YOU DO THIS TOO ME,4 YEARS OF MARRIAGE I HAVE GIVEN YOU EVERYTHING,AND THIS IS HOW YOU DO ME ? YOU CHEAT ON ME? HE WALKED INSIDE OUR HOUSE IN RAGE HE BEGAN PACKING HIS BELONGINGS AND SHOUTING AT ME, YOU ARE THE ONE ALWAYS FUSSING ABOUT STAY OUT OF OTHER WOMAN FACES AND YOU GO DO THIS? HE WAS ABOUT TO HIT ME BECAUSE OF THE HURT OF MY CONFESSING MY UNFAITHFULNESS WAS JUST OVERWHELMING TO HIM HE NEVER WOULD HAVE THOUGHT I COULD DO SUCH A THING TO HIM.

I ASKED MY HUSBAND TO CALM DOWN AND SIT DOWN SO WE CAN TALK ABOUT IT, HE ASKED ME WHO IS IT? WHO HAVE YOU BEEN UNFAITHFUL WITH? WE BOTH CRIED TOGETHER I EMBRACED HIM AND CRIED WITH HIM BUT IT WAS STILL A RAGE, HE ASKED ME AGAIN WHO IS IT? WHO IS THIS PUNK? DO HE KNOW YOU ARE MARRIED? DO HE KNOW ABOUT ME? HAVE YOU TOLD HIM ABOUT ME? HE SNATCHED MY PHONE AND SAID HE WILL KNOW ABOUT ME TODAY, AND BEGAN TO LOOK THROUGH MY PHONE LOOKING FOR PICTURES AND NUMBERS AND TEXT MESSAGES, HE GAVE ME MY PHONE BACK AND SAID CALL HIM,SHOW ME A PICTURE OF HIM, YOU MIDAS WELL YOU WERE BOLD ENOUGH TO TELL ME ABOUT THIS MAN SO SHOW ME WHO HE IS, I KINDLY PULLED UP THE PICTURE AND SHOWED IT TO MY HUSBAND SAYING THIS IS THE MAN I HAVE BEEN UNFAITHFUL WITH.... AS I GAVE HIM MY PHONE, HE LOOKED AT THE PHONE AND SAW A PICTURE OF HIMSELF AND SAID: WHAT? THIS IS ME ARE YOU BEING SMART RIGHT NOW ARE YOU PLAYING ON MY INTELLIGENCE RIGHT NOW? BECAUSE RIGHT NOW IS NOT THE TIME, I SAID TO HIM I KNOW BABY RIGHT NOW IS NOT THE TIME AND BEFORE YOU WALK OUT THAT DOOR, I HAVE BEEN HONEST WITH YOU FROM THE START OF THIS CONFESSION, AND YES IT IS YOU,

I HAVE BEEN UNFAITHFUL WITH YOU,,, I HAVE BEEN UNFAITHFUL WITH GOD BECAUSE I HAVE BEEN SO BUSY LOVING YOU. I HAVE BEEN WORKING SO HARD BEING A GOOD WIFE, TO THAT I FORGOT ABOUT GOD. MY HUSBAND WALKED TO THE PATIO DOOR AND GAZED OUT IN SUCH A DISSARAY, I TOLD HIM I KNOW HOW YOU MUST FEEL BUT YOU CANT IMAGINE HOW I MUST FEEL, BECAUSE WHEN I MET YOU I WAS SO DEDICATED TO GOD DEDICATED TO MY WALK AND VERY DEDICATED IN MY ASSIGNMENT FROM GOD WHICH IS MY MODEL DANCE AND PRAISE MENTORING PROGRAM, I WAS SO DEVOTED TO GOD, AND YOU SAID THAT WHAT YOU WERE ALWAYS LOOKING FOR WAS A SAVED WOMAN, AND THAT ONE OF THE REASONS YOU WANTED TO MARRY ME AND WOULDN'T TAKE MY NO AS AN ANSWER. YOU WOULD TELL ME HOW MUCH YOU LOVE AND RESPECT

MY WALK WITH GOD. I FELL FOR THE GODLY MAN YOU BETRAYED TO BE WHEN WE MET, I ENJOYED US PRAYING TOGETHER AND GOING TO CHURCH TOGETHER IT WAS SO NICE TO SHARE THE WORD OF GOD WITH SOMEONE WHO SHARED THE SAME WALKS OF LIFE AND THAT WAS LOVING GOD. I HAD PROMISED GOD TEN YEARS AGO THAT I WOULD COMPLETE HIS ASSIGNMENT ON MY LIFE IF ITS THE LITTLE GIRLS I WILL MENTOR LEAD LOVE AND GUIDE THEM INTO GOD HANDS, AND NOTHING WOULD STOP ME I LOVE MY GOD THAT MUCH AND GOD TRUSTED ME TO DO THE JOB, MY OTHER BUSINESS DID WELL YOU DID WELL ON YOUR JOB WE WERE BEING BLESSED, GOD HAD BLESSED ME, AND BLESSED MY HOME, AND BLESSED MY KIDS DAY IN AND DAY OUT "BUT" I BELIEVED I WAS BLESSED WITH A GOOD HUSBAND, AS I BEGAN TO FALL IN LOVE WITH YOU, AS I BEGAN TO ENJOY TRAVELING WITH YOU, AS I BEGAN SHOPPING AND LIVING IT UP WITH YOU, YOU SHATTERED ME WITH EVERYTHING, WE GOT MARRIED AND IT FELT PERFECT IN THE BEGINNING . BECAUSE WE WOULD GO TO CHURCH TOGETHER, PRAY TOGETHER STUDY THE BIBLE TOGETHER, BUT SLOWLY, WE STOPPED LIVING BY THE WORD WE HEARD ON SUNDAY. WE STARTED WORSHIPING MONEY AND MATERIAL THINGS, WE FOUND OUR CHRISTIAN FRIENDS BORING, SO WE CHANGED OUR CIRCLE OF FRIENDS,. AND LOOK AT US NOW, WE LIVE IN A NICE PLACE BUT GOD IS NOT THERE,YOU BEGAN TAKING ME TO UNGODLY PLACES TO HAVE FUN, I BEGAN TO WATCH YOU DRINK TOO MUCH AND I WANTED TO FEEL GOOD WITH YOU SO I BEGAN TO TAKE THE OFFERS FROM YOU TO DRINK WINE WINE AND MORE WINE, IN ORDER TO PLEASE YOU.I WAS WILLING TO PROVE TO YOU THAT I WAS A GOOD WIFE AND NOT THAT AS YOU WOULD SAY TO ME A HOLY ROLELY, IT WAS LIKE I WAS BLINDED BY LOVE, I WOULDN'T CONFRONT YOU WHEN YOU STARTED TO GO ASTRAY AND I BEGAN WATCHING YOU GO ASTRAY EVERY 90 DAYS I WOULD TRY TO PULL YOU BACK TO GOD BUT AFTER SO LONG I GOT LOST WITH YOU AND STOPPED TRYING TO PULL YOU BACK TO GOD, I WAS LOST SO LOST AND CONFUSED AND BEGAN TO GET ANGRY WITH GOD AND ASK WHY ? I WAS SO LOST THAT I BECAME PROUD SHALLOW AND SELF CENTERED, ALL WHILE THINKING IM BEING A GOOD WIFE, ALL WHILE SAYING THIS IS NOT ME ANYMORE, I HAVE CHANGED SO MUCH FROM THE WOMAN YOU MET. WE BOTH HAVE CHANGED. WE HAVE IT ALL A NICE HOME, WE EAT GOOD MEALS, WE MAKE GOOD MONEY WE HAVE A COMFORTABLE LIFE, ALL OF THIS GOODNESS MADE US FORGET ABOUT GOD, THE GOD WHO GAVE US ALL OF THIS. I AM NOTHING WITHOUT GOD AND I FEEL ASHAMED THAT I HAVE ABANDONED THE GOD RESPONSIBLE FOR ALL I AM AND HAVE. WE HAVE STARTED HAVING PROBLEMS IN OUR MARRIAGE, BECAUSE GOD IS NO LONGER BUILDING OUR LOVE, WE ARE DOING IT ON OUR OWN AND WE ARE FAILING. I WANT TO GO BACK TO THE WOMAN I USED TO BE I MISS ME, A WOMAN OF GOD A WOMAN AFTER GODS OWN HEART, I MISS THE PEACE I HAD, I MISS FEELING BLESSED,I MISSED PRAYING WITH YOU, I MISS YOU SEEKING GODS FACE,I MISSED YOU ASKING ME TO PRAY WITH YOU AND TO READ THE BIBLE WITH YOU,, WHAT DOES IT PROFIT ME TO GAIN THE WORLD BUT LOOSE MY SOUL AND IN OUR CASE WHAT DOES IT PROFIT US TO GAIN A BEAUTIFUL MARRIAGE YET LOOSE OUR SOULS, I AM GOING BACK TO GOD. ONLY AS A WIFE SUBMITTED TO GOD WILL I BE THE BEST WIFE TO YOU.

HE WHO FINDS A WIFE FINDS A GOOD THING AND OBTAIN FAVOR FROM GOD, BUT I CAN NOT BRING FAVOUR TO YOU IF I CONTINUE BEING DISCONNECTED FROM

GOD. I NEED MY SPIRITUAL LIFE BACK. I NEED GOD BACK IN OUR HOME AND IN OUR MARRIAGE, MY HUSBAND BEGAN TO CRY AND SAID HE WAS SO SORRY HE HUGGED ME TIGHT AND WE CRIED TOGETHER HE CRIED OUT I AM SO SORRY I AM SORRY FOR GOING ASTRAY AND TAKING YOU WITH ME I HAVE A PROBLEM THAT I HAVE TO GIVE TO GOD SO HE CAN DELIVER ME, I AM SO SORRY, BECAUSE YOU CHOSE TO MARRY ME BECAUSE YOU THOUGHT YOU WERE MARRYING A GOOD MAN A GOD FEARING MAN, MARRIAGE SHOULDN'T BE A STUMBLING A BLOCK IN OUR WALK WITH GOD . THE THOUGHT OF YOU CHEATING ON ME WAS UNBEARABLE IT HURT ME SO BAD. I CANT EVEN BEGAN TO THINK HOW GOD FEELS WHEN WE ARE UNFAITHFUL TO HIM.GOD HAVE BLESSED US WITH ALL WE WANTED AN THIS IS HOW WE REPAY HIM, AT THE THOUGHT OF YOU CHEATING ON ME LEFT ME IN A RAGE YET GOD PATIENTLY LOOKS AT US IN OUR UNFAITHFULNESS DESIRING US TO GO BACK TO HIM. I MY HUSBAND SAID I WAN T TO GO BACK TOO. I WANT MORE IN MY LIFE THAN THESE EARTHLY THINGS, I WANT GOD. I AM SO SORRY FOR SHOUTING AT YOU; I LOVE YOU. AND I KNOW NOW WE CAN'T MAKE IT WITHOUT GOD, LORD WE THANK YOU FOR REVEALING, REPLACING, REMOVING, RENEWING AND REBUILDING OUR LIVES.

My Photo Gallery Reflects Life, Peace, Joy, And Happiness Before My 19 But Not 20. And This Is Why I Chose Me

Printed in the United States
by Baker & Taylor Publisher Services